STRAVINSKY AT REHEARSAL

STRAVINSKY
AT REHEARSAL

A Sketchbook by
Milein Cosman

with text by
Hans Keller

LONDON : DENNIS DOBSON

First published in Great Britain 1962 by Dobson Books Ltd
80 Kensington Church Street, London W8
and printed by Metcalfe & Co Ltd, Cambridge

ACKNOWLEDGMENTS

All these drawings were done at rehearsals for BBC concerts which Stravinsky conducted in 1958, 1959 and 1961, including a concert performance of "Oedipus Rex" in 1959 with Cocteau as speaker; hence, and because of his long association with Stravinsky, Cocteau's presence in this book.

I should like to thank the BBC for their hospitality and Mr. William Glock for the loan of his drawings. Above all, I would thank Stravinsky himself for being, rather like Venice, an ever-changing delight to the eye, unaware of its intrusion.

M.C.

I would like to express my thanks to Messrs. Faber and Faber for permission to quote from MEMORIES AND COMMENTARIES by Igor Stravinsky and Robert Craft.

H.K.

STRAVINSKY AT REHEARSAL

Across the divisions of style, beyond the wars of musical 'schools', the rival symptoms and rival claims of creative inferiority feelings (unconfessed or at least semi-conscious); across all artificial curtains that separate the seeming irreconcilables of our disunited musical world, there cuts one straight division, the most recent and the most real of them all: the iron curtain between physical and phoney creativity. Not that the physical is the 'A' and 'O' of music; but it certainly is the 'A'.

The division was unimaginable so long as there were only musical composers. But once the crumbling of tonality had removed that common background, intuitively comprehensible in terms of sound alone, against which everybody composed, once backgrounds began to vary from composer to composer, making comprehension proportionately more difficult, the road was open to a confusion between the as yet uncomprehended and the necessarily incomprehensible—necessarily, inasmuch as it does not make sense as sound.

Today, we are quite often confronted with unmusical composers producing non-sounding sense; that they cheat their audiences is only incidental to their cheating themselves about their senseless sounds, which they themselves only 'understand' because they know the soundless sense behind, or rather beside the music. They are on the wrong side of the iron curtain. There are others, however, whose very heart is torn asunder by the iron curtain, with one half on the right side, the other under the dictatorship of soundless intellectualism, musically atrophied. They present the newest and greatest problem of musical culture, for some of our intensest talents are among them. There are only a handful whose heart is altogether pure, unharmed, untouched by the iron curtain which, with inexorable regularity, is drawn up for a fleeting moment and then crashes down again, hitting all but these very few.

Which few? For the duration of our musical crisis, a new, empirical criterion for the existence of genius seems to be emerging. It is only the geniuses amongst the composers writing in a contemporary idiom who retain their musicality uncorrupted, making sense of sound and of nothing alse. They may make curious bedfellows—Schoenberg, Stravinsky, Britten, Skalkottas, Shostakovitch—but even though they may not know it, their hearts are united in sounding logic, and the sense behind their music (if you can so separate a sense that can only be musically expressed) is spiritual rather than intellectual—a message, revelation, or both, according to the character of the composer.

As time progresses, strange bedfellows get used to each other, not just through habit, but by discovering the affinities which made them bedfellows in the first place—or, if they do not live to see their unity, posterity sees it for them. Two of my five geniuses are dead; one of them, the father of our musical age, did not live to see the influence he was to exert on what he would have regarded as the most unlikely recipients of his thoughts—Britten and Stravinsky. His influence on Britten is relatively superficial, more psychological than musical, but in Stravinsky, Schoenberg's twelve-tone method eventually produced one of those profound changes of creative mind of which no other great creator, with the possible exception of Picasso, has ever been capable.

When Theodor Adorno, our age's musical philosopher-in-chief, wrote his *Philosophy of New Music* in 1949, he was still able to play off Schoenberg against Stravinsky, whose music he then regarded as a death-mask of the past (my metaphor); in fact, the whole book develops in the field of tension created by the polarity Adorno postulated between Schoenberg and Stravinsky. Admittedly, at that stage, as indeed for decades before, the two composers represented the fundamental stylistic division of our age, and when I said at the time that they had something more basic in common than many Stravinskyians on the one hand and Schoenbergians on the other (to wit, music), my argument seemed tenuous: there were not many who shared my admiration for either composer. But then, in the twenties, more than two decades before I came in, a seemingly elemental historical clash had occurred: while Stravinsky, via neo-classicism, was diving into the past, Schoenberg, via the tone-row, was jumping into the future. So violent a contrast was too much for the composers themselves to bear: they theorized against each other, or justified themselves against each other, and though in later years they calmed down and re-realized that music was music, their ambivalent attitudes towards each other never quite left them.

How then, in the circumstances, was it possible for Stravinsky to turn serial in the fifties and sixties, at first cautiously and indeed tonally, later downright twelve-tonally and even, in the *Movements* for piano and orchestra, atonally, making nonsense of Adorno's nowise senseless basic thesis? Even for an admirer of both composers, Stravinsky's absorption of Schoenberg's technique was arguably the profoundest surprise in the history of music.

With the help of psychological insight on the one hand and musical insight on the other, it should be possible to explain the latest development of this most puzzling of all great composers—most puzzling because truly unprecedented.

All good composers start out from the past; they normally come to create against its background. Most bad composers remain stuck in it and are therefore compelled to use it as a foreground: to copy it. Stravinsky is the first great composer who has it both ways: he keeps his past, or rather his pasts, in the glaring foreground, yet composes against them, or, if you like, through them. Anybody can twist a diatonic harmony, but only Stravinsky can re-characterize it by the addition of a wrong note or two.

Apropos of his treatment of Pergolesi's melodies in the ballet *Pulcinella* (1919-20), at that cataclysmic moment when he confronted

Schoenberg across a wider and steeper precipice than any faced by any two artists at any time, Stravinsky asked: 'Should my line of action be dominated by my love or by my respect for Pergolesi's music? Is it love or respect that urges us to possess a woman? Is it not by love alone that we succeed in penetrating to the very essence of a being? But then, does love diminish respect? Respect alone remains barren and can never serve as a productive or creative factor. In order to create, there must be a creative force, and what force is more potent than love?' He felt his 'conscience to be innocent of sacrilege'; indeed, he considered that his attitude towards Pergolesi was 'the only possible one towards the music of earlier ages'. For 'love' read 'hate' without excluding love: we shall see at once precisely why.

We recall Stravinsky's suggestion that 'rape may be justified by the creation of a child'. Paul Valéry changed the metaphor: 'A lion consists of digested lambs'. Now, psychoanalysis recognizes two basic types of love, self-love apart. Genetically the more primitive is identification, which stems from the earliest, sucking stage of infancy and whose prototype is oral incorporation—hence the technical term 'introjection' for the 'absorption of the environment into the personality' (Ernest Jones); hence, too, Valéry's metaphor. The other type, 'object love', is what we commonly understand by love. In monosyllables, identification is based on the need to *be* someone, object love on the need to *have* someone. Identification, more elemental, is the more ambivalent of the two, the more aggressive: for one thing you destroy what you eat, for another you want to replace the person you want to be.

Ordinary artistic development always starts with identification: while the composer's own creative ego is still weak, he identifies himself with his teachers and with older masters and proceeds to imitate them. This is the stage where the past, his future background, is still in the foreground of his creative thought. As his originality grows

4

with the maturation of his creative personality, those father figures are absorbed by the composer's artistic conscience and recede into the background. Once maturity is reached, and if no creative trauma lies in wait for him (such as the encounter with Bach which Mozart had to face as a mature genius), his creative 'love relations' with other composers amount to no more than sporadic flirtations resulting in, say, variations on another composer's theme: these are the children of 'object love' rather than of identification.

Alone amongst geniuses, again with the possible exception of Picasso, Stravinsky has actually developed his capacity for identification together with the unfolding of his intense originality. At the same time, as his commentary on *Pulcinella* indicates, his creative mind also employs a good deal of highly aggressive 'object love' ('rape may be justified by the creation of a child'): he makes the aggressive best of both love worlds, though identification remains the basic 'dynamic force'. No previous composer has shown any desire to compose his way 'into the very essence of a being'.

> And all men kill the thing they love,
> By all let this be heard,
> Some do it with a bitter look,
> Some with a flattering word,
> The coward does it with a kiss,
> The brave man with a sword!

There is some special pleading here, but there is a truth too. Stravinsky has in fact himself employed the bitter look, the flattering word, and the sword, but he has never killed the past by kissing it, as so many of his followers and all pure neo-classicists have done.

Consider such a spotless and gigantic masterpiece as the *Symphony of Psalms* (1930), where identifications with the past span a wide field, stretching back into the archaic: when the opening four-part fugue of the second movement (with the answer in the dominant) raises its voice through what we might call the life-mask of Bach, we realize that the term 'neo-classicism' is no longer good enough.

Psychologically, the chief fascination of the *Symphony of Psalms* is the nature of its profound expressiveness. That is to say, the work is expressive through the very suppression of expressionism, through that in-turned, self-castigating aggression which prompted Adorno and myself, independently, to describe it as sado-masochistic. I have been heavily criticized for this characterization; my simple reply is that it is not a devaluation. What it does signify is the complexity of Stravinsky's creative aggression, which manifests itself in his aggressive love and aggressive self-love. Stravinsky's genius has utilized its sado-masochism, i.e. both its aggression turned inwards and its enjoyment of such self-attack, towards his unique, tense, meaning-laden suppressionism. His anti-expressionism does not however, as Adorno thinks, result in emptiness, but in fullness fully opposed, in a state of statically intense tension, of dynamic staticism.

The outstanding common trait of Stravinsky's successive styles is indeed their self-restrictive tendency. In point of fact, his urge towards formal stringency and simplicity might well be considered to go beyond the requirements of unity and clarity: he does not discipline his inspiration; rather, he is more lavishly inspired by self-discipline than any other composer—even today, when creators, robbed of universally valid disciplines and afraid of their undesired freedom, tend to be obsessed with self-disciplinary measures as a matter of pathological course. The source of Stravinsky's self-restrictiveness is not only his in-turned aggression, but also his need for creative identification: identifications with other styles automatically impose severe limitations upon the imagination.

It is in the light of this psychological background, then, that Stravinsky's amazing change of mind towards serialism has to be examined. Now, the simplest, and perhaps the most important fact about his

6

gradual conversion is its chronology: it all happened after Schoenberg's death—we might almost say, by way of creative mourning. Ever since 1916, when Freud published his *Mourning and Melancholia*, we have come to understand that what he called the 'identification of the ego with the lost object' is at the root of all mourning: in concentrated fashion, that very process of 'introjection' takes place which, as we have seen, forms part and parcel of Stravinsky's creative character anyhow.

Grief-inspired incorporations, once our attention is drawn to them, are readily observable by the naked eye. They are especially impressive where the mourned person was a creative or public figure with well-defined, widely familiar character traits: we can all think of more than one widow who was inwardly compelled to burden her psyche with her famous husband's peculiarities, however eccentric, and to act out what she understood to be his role. Even on a social scale, the phenomenon makes itself easily felt when a personality dies whose work is hotly contested: public reactions veer in his favour, he is accepted as 'one of us', and unfavourable critics 'introject' him to the extent of turning into advocates. In fact, in the case of Schoenberg himself, while we who had always pleaded for his music prided ourselves on the eventual success of our endeavours, there is little doubt that when it came to it, psychology achieved what we hadn't. A comparison between some of our leading critics' writings before and after his death makes downright grotesque reading: an imaginary public was chided for the critic's own past attitudes.

Stravinsky's character being predestined to identifications with, incorporations of the past, it is not, perhaps, quite so mysterious any more that he naturally availed himself of the mourning mechanisms as soon as Schoenberg had become a thing of the past. At the same time, we must, I think, beware of facile explanations: the psychological situation is not as simple as all that. For one thing, why should

Stravinsky mourn Schoenberg anyway? A condition of mourning is a fairly high minimum of love, the aggressive side of the picture being usually hidden from superficial inspection. With Stravinsky, on the other hand, we need not seek for the aggression; it is the love aspect of which we cannot find much trace. There is no positive evidence that deep love was lost between the two composers; when they landed in Hollywood, they did not venture near each other. In a sense, they must have disliked each other more generously than some music critics disliked both of them, for they were, after all, composers of diametrically opposite orientation, with a corresponding creative intensity behind their mutual dislike. Assuming, however, that there was more mutual love or respect than met the eye (and there is some evidence of suppressed admiration), the proportionate guilt reaction on Schoenberg's death would help Stravinsky towards that state of creative mourning. But it wouldn't be enough. Our psychological budget is still unbalanced; our explanation remains artificial so long as we do not find further items on the credit side of Stravinsky's most revolutionary identification, be they purely psychological, musical, or both.

Facts are better than theories, and nothing is more foolish than not to be wise after the event. Let us look at the precise nature and circumstances of Stravinsky's introjection of Schoenberg's method, as well as at his own attitude towards his change of direction, in order to discover more concretely how it came about. The first thing that strikes us, however, is a further element of confusion, a further inconsistency. Whereas, especially in their early stages, Stravinsky's serial ventures were stressedly Schoenbergian in technical approach, his public utterances have almost throughout exalted Webern at the expense of Schoenberg, the implication being that he actually 'had it' from Webern, the real father of the future—a status accorded to this great minor master by current *avant-gardist* opinion. To my mind, this contradiction reached its manifest climax on a private occasion. In the early stages of Stravinsky's serial technique, when the news had reached the musical world that he admired Webern enormously, I wrote an article for a musical journal, entitled *In Memoriam Dylan Thomas: Stravinsky's Schoenbergian Technique*, and containing a complete analysis of his Dylan Thomas dirge. Explicitly and implicitly, I showed that the strictly serial piece, though based on a five-note row, applied Schoenberg's own serial concept very conscientiously. The then editor of the journal, for reasons which need not concern us here but of which I approved, sent a proof of the article to the composer before it was published. It came back with stressedly appreciative marginal comments, and without a word of criticism. At the same time, on more public occasions, Stravinsky made his indebtedness to Webern ever clearer—and his ambivalence towards Schoenberg too. There are passages in Robert Craft's *Conversations with Stravinsky* which make one seriously wonder whether the composer really had a proper look at all the Schoenberg works he criticizes (he certainly cannot have heard them all), though in order to keep his ambivalence as tidy as possible in his difficult psychological circumstances, he reserves his most whole-hearted and general condemnation for Schoenberg's literary output: 'Schoenberg's work has too many inequalities for us to embrace it as a whole. For example, nearly all of his texts are appallingly bad, some of them so bad as to discourage performance of the music.' As a matter of fact, German-speaking countries acknowledged Schoenberg's great literary gifts decades before they recognized his musical genius; while nowadays, his texts are even appreciated by foreigners, by critics within Stravinsky's own cultural orbit: 'What is so striking [about *Moses and Aron*] is the enormous significance of the libretto and its unusual form. This text is concentrated to an extreme degree. Psychologically as well as dramatically and ethically, it is of a compactness which we never encounter in the realm of opera. There is no padding

9

here, there are none of the *clichés* with which operatic texts commonly abound. . . . It is a fact that Schoenberg has found a remarkable balance between the literary and the musical elements of his work'. Thus Claude Rostand.

But while Stravinsky's opinions of Schoenberg oscillate between extremes, Webern cannot put a foot wrong—be it Webern the composer or Webern the man. In fact, Stravinsky's eulogy on Webern in the second batch of conversations between him and Robert Craft (*Memories and Commentaries*) prompted Peter J. Pirie to the somewhat despairing observation that he could not make up his mind 'about the exact intellectual stature of a man who . . . sentimentalizes like a teenager over Webern. . .' I dislike this kind of description of a genius's reaction to a near-genius, but the very fact that a by no means insensitive critic was driven to it is an indication of the intensity and purity of Stravinsky's admiration for Webern. There is only one parallel, an acutely striking one, to this kind of public propaganda, on the part of a genius, for a dead master: Schoenberg's own memorial lecture on *Gustav Mahler* (1912), translated and reprinted in *Style and Idea*. The history of Schoenberg's relation to Mahler is itself one of passionate ambivalence, and the lecture is a guilt reaction if ever there was one, 'mourning and melancholia' *par excellence*.

What I had to introduce as an element of confusion, the seemingly impenetrable cloud hanging over Stravinsky's 'true' feelings about Schoenberg and Webern, seems to turn into the first step towards the solution of our problem. My metaphor is carefully mixed: the cloud is substantial, solid: we may step on it and look beyond. The fact is that all feelings are 'true', and if they contradict each other they are all the truer, stronger: if either side isn't strong, it gives in and is liquidated. Stravinsky's unconscious was prepared to incorporate and mourn Schoenberg on condition that Webern could be absorbed at the same time, and that the manifestly aggressive side of the psychological deal could be confined to Schoenberg, so that Webern could bathe in Schoenberg's glory as well as his own.

Our next and final two steps seem now clearly marked. We have to find out what made it possible for Stravinsky to be attracted by Webern to such an extent, and what made it necessary to retain Schoenberg.

Now it so happens that apart from Stravinsky himself, Webern is the only great sado-masochistic figure in the history of music. In his case, masochism and in-turned sadism are markedly stronger than in Stravinsky's; self-restrictiveness turns into self-destruction. What I mean is that Webern has been misunderstood by his followers with such absolute consistency that we must make him at least partly responsible for this historical, and by now historic misapprehension: it is as if he had worked towards being killed after his death. At the present juncture in the development of composition, the prestige of his work depends in fact on the suppression of that which it expresses or purports to express, namely, emotion. Urged on by his masochism, Webern drove his heart-felt *espressivo* style beyond the extremes of compression towards partial or sometimes wholesale suppression. With Stravinsky, such suppression is suppressionism: it is artistically intended and hence functional, i.e. itself expressive. With Webern it is unintentional, accidental from the artistic point of view, though essential psychologically. In that sense, Webern's art is pathological, neurotic, whereas Stravinsky's isn't. Neurosis is unrealism; in art, it is a failure of adjustment to psychic reality. Inasmuch as Webern did not say what he had to say and what he thought he was saying, and inasmuch as this was not due to technical deficiencies (which, in my view, it virtually never was), he was a neurotic master (the only one in our history apart from Brahms who tended to deny his feelings when he became afraid of them, fearing them to be 'sentimental').

It can easily be seen that Stravinsky would be gladly prepared to

11

swallow (incorporate) this sado-masochistic character if he did not have
to swallow it whole. Let us be a little more concrete and turn to the
musical effects of Webern's sado-masochism—his sparse, ultra-trans-
parent textures, cleaner, it must be said, than anything our entire
musical history had had to offer until then. Once Stravinsky was
incorporating the twelve-tone method, which itself offers many self-
restrictive possibilities to those (and only to those) who want them,
once his hostility towards atonality was on the wane, Webern's textures
must have exercised a particular fascination on the suppressionist: it
is one of the supreme paradoxes of musical history, as indeed of history
in general, that pathology can produce health. (The opposite, alas, is
also true, as can be observed in the Nazi interpretations of Wagner,
Nietzsche, and even Bruckner.) If Webern was ever capable of musical
development—in healthy circumstances one of the inevitable conse-
quences of an *espressivo* style—his sado-masochism soon drove the
capacity out of his system; and Stravinsky, the anti-expressionist and
professed anti-developer *par excellence*, must have been happy to hear
the unfinished result—unfinished because the twelve-tone method, a
developmental procedure if ever there was one, suppresses itself in
Webern's work. How Stravinsky managed to use the method undam-
aged, yet undeveloping, remains one of the miracles of genius; but one
thing is certain—that he could not have done so without, on the one
hand, his absolute loyalty to physical musical reality, to sounding sense,
and on the other (or not so other) hand, Schoenberg's help.

We thus come to the last step in our investigation. When every-
thing psychological is said and done, what was it in Schoenberg's own
twelve-tone method that attracted Stravinsky so intensely and lastingly
that it made all the psychological complications we have described
worth while? And even on the assumption of a topically favourable
psychological climate such as I have outlined, of potent stimuli towards
identification exciting this perpetually identifying creative character,

what was it, musically, that overcame a life-time of musical resistance, an era of official musical polarity? Had Stravinsky 'killed the thing he loved', had he treated Schoenberg's twelve-tone method as savagely as Webern treated his own, our explanation would not be far to seek; it could, in fact, remain on the psychological level. But he didn't. On the contrary, with the exception of Nikos Skalkottas and the partial exception of Roberto Gerhard, Schoenberg's method has not, to date, found as realistic a follower as Stravinsky.

So far, when speaking about twelve-tone technique, I have kept my remarks general, hoping that they would so make essential sense to the uninitiated, while the versed would pin them down to the relevant concrete details. When explaining Schoenberg's specific attraction for Stravinsky, however, I shall have to be mildly technical, without, however, saying anything that presupposes a great deal of technical knowledge.

While for Webern the tone-row is usually abstract, which is to say that it does not readily crystallize into something of melodic significance and therefore remains largely inaudible, the Schoenbergian tone-row is *abstracted from a melodic idea*, an initial inspiration: by and large, it *is* this idea without its rhythm—a succession of notes derived from a tune, and uncommitted to the rhythm of the tune: my term for it is 'sub-thematic'. It may be a little longer than the tune, in which case the rest of the row may be used towards the continuation; or it may be a bit shorter than the tune, in which case the tune will comprise more than one rotation of the row. In any case, however, the characteristic trait of the Schoenbergian row is its original concreteness—its function as a melodic motif, retaining its melodic aspect even when it is divested of its rhythm, or rather, when endowed with a new rhythm. It is due to the melodic idea from which it springs, and the melodic quality which it therefore retains, that the Schoenbergian row is ultimately and spontaneously audible.

The vast majority of serial composers evince exactly the opposite approach—an approach to which Webern inclined, without however fully subscribing to it. With them, the serial idea, the idea of a particular series or a special kind of series, comes first, and the music afterwards. The more pronouncedly phoney ones among them have even gone so far as to write of Schoenberg's rows contemptuously as 'music-making rows' (*Musizierreihen*), comparing them unfavourably with their own 'structural' rows. I cannot explain to the reader what exactly a 'structural' row is, or why it is more structural than a 'music-making' row, because I have never understood the term myself; suffice it to say that you don't know a structural row when you hear it.

Now, what drew Stravinsky to Schoenberg's method, despite the vast difference in compositorial outlook between the two, was, I suggest, its 'music-making' significance. I have pointed again and again to this, as it seems to me, obvious trait of Stravinsky's serial technique, long before he did so himself. When he finally did (in *Memories and Commentaries*), he made no mention, of course, of Schoenberg, but the way in which he described his technique left no more doubt about the correctness of my diagnosis. The crucial passage runs as follows:

Robert Craft: Would you analyse your own composing process in any part of one of your more recent pieces—in, for example, the little *Epitaphium*?

Stravinsky: I began the *Epitaphium* with the flute-clarinet duet. . . . In the manner I have described in our previous conversations I heard and composed a melodic-harmonic phrase. I certainly did not (and never do) begin with a purely serial idea and, in fact, when I began I did not know, or care, whether all twelve notes would be used. After I had written about half the first phrase I saw its serial pattern, however, and then perhaps I began to work towards that pattern. The constructive problem that first attracted me in the two-part counterpoint of the first phrase was the harmonic one of minor seconds.

Compare this with Schoenberg's categorical statement in a letter to Josef Rufer (quoted in the latter's *Composition with Twelve Notes*; the translation is mine): 'The original idea of a row always occurs to me in the form of a thematic character'.

The road to our understanding is clear. Across the divisions of style, beyond the wars of their schools, Stravinsky and Schoenberg eventually met on the basis of concrete, audible, sounding sense. By way of creative mourning, Stravinsky, who had always tended towards ambivalent identification, became aware of the concrete possibilities in Schoenberg's method and proceeded to incorporate it, insisting on getting Webern into the bargain. With the unerring certainty of genius, he split his mourning attitude between the two composers (some of his remarks about Webern sound as if the Schoenberg pupil had died yesterday) and took from either what he needed, leaving the unrealistic aspects of Webern as well as the developmental and expressionist aspects of Schoenberg on one side. Fascinated, yet uncorrupted, by some of the most recent, partly un-sounding developments of musical composition, he continues to make sense of sound and of nothing else, an advanced aim to those whom even he regards as more advanced than himself. Look after the physical reality of your music, he tells them, and the spirit will look after itself. Unlike them, he is not an arm-chair composer; he remains what this book shows him to be—a music-maker.

Cocteau